WWW.FARWESTPRESS.COM

FIRST EDITION

ISBN 978-1-7365388-5-2

PRINTED IN THE UNITED STATES OF AMERICA

THE **BABA** BOOKS/
ANIMAL MY SOUL

FOR ANYONE WHO IS
UNSATISFIED WITH
THEIR LIFE
STORY AND
FORGETS THAT
THE

AUTHOR IS
ENTITLED TO REWRITE
THE WHOLE THING

YOU BIG LIBERATOR

...

For the young dads, all broke down with no pots to piss in
And broke souls who claim wealth, yet buy only what gets sold

...

For the free souls you cage in and bind tight
And their hands that play tricks to trapped eyes!

To flip lids like teen jesus! and ole bums who pave shits in gold streets - believing and knowing they're god

...

...

For the zip tied tongues and zip locked lives
carved in hollow wood, wrapped in plastic
Be free
You are allowed.
You're pissing off the environment - Also, people

For people!

...

For old dads with punched clocks and lost time
who feel short - stand up, you live forever

...

For your mom, the saint patron of good god
and blind faith and sharp tongues that cut down
dreams
only to test em' -
They make belief

...

...

For young moms who fight fear with sharp
thoughts of what cuts and dulls lives
Drop the axe, see the bleeding hearts
Believe yours

...

For our kids who refuse to believe a shadow isn't
cast away by light
And don't think to save worlds,
do

...

...

For my heroes who all died in small ways
at some point this past life, who still live
but as peers
who take shits too

...

For my fears
You have taught me well and
I will not mourn your passing

...

...

And for you, who see power as possession
And for you, who seek nothing you can't see
And for you, who can't stand to sit naked
And for those always right · bound to fall
for what's left

What's left?

...

...

...

For the tower we've built and won't miss
With self portraits and torn frames that line walls
with broke selves, good riddance

...

And for you, who can be so scared and so afraid
I see you, of course
I see me!

For those who don't know that we too
are all of these things

Come on out and see the nothing we've been
afraid of

...

It took a long time to get to here
Past the shoeless trip 'long the glasslined path

...

But here we are now

AND MAY IT PLEASE BE UGLY

...

Fate had it out for me that you would show up
right on time. You weren't pretty or anything at
all. You were nothing. And you stuck around.
I know you.
Stick around -

...

I know things don't have to be pretty to give you
life or break your heart. My best teachers were
ugly, vile things - coaxing me to see different. Sit-
ting me down, shouting at me to stand up with my
imagination. Run wild and come and kiss me
familiar stranger. I did. I died.
Still here.
Stick around -

...

I can write pretty and well and I went to school and
all. But I know the pretty and well of this world and
they have only taught me deceit. Sure, they taught
me, but nothing was a more consistent teacher.
And at least nothing was honest.
So here's some raw text -

...

...

I've been writing and writing and transcribing and
scanning and stopping and starting, thinkin'
There's an awful amount of pretty in the world.
BUT YOU KNOW THE WORLD, don't ya??
Yeah you do...and we're all owed a little bit of that
mess. The mess that liberates. The mess that frees
us all up...

...

/Beat 1
If a tree gets chopped in the woods at Toluca Lake -
everyone hears. Nobody does a damn thing.

...

/Beat 2
A woman lost her dog today to a coyote and cried
bloody murder for fifteen minutes straight and all
my neighbors took baths in warm water.
They know nothing.
But not like me. And not like you.
It can be so beautiful.

...
There is only nothing to be afraid of
Give a kiss
Help a stranger and don't act
Like you've never lost a dog before.

...

Give me ugly animals and lost dogs and sunbeat bums and wayward children and real love. Real love! All sick and tired...and honest, at least. Or give me nothing.

...

To the publisher:
Willie,
I became so obsessed by the idea of this thing.
I removed myself from the world entirely.
Becoming obsessed is one way to try and
withdraw from the world. It is one way to turn
away from the imagined horrors of a life lived
honestly. However in doing so, one opts out of
the ecstasies as well. This type of thing seems
prohibited in good writing. This has become
evident to the nth degree as I move woefully
deeper into excavating these past years, these
past journals. Within them lies revelation, with-
in them lies terror.
But the book, now books…they are in there too.
Best,
Joseph

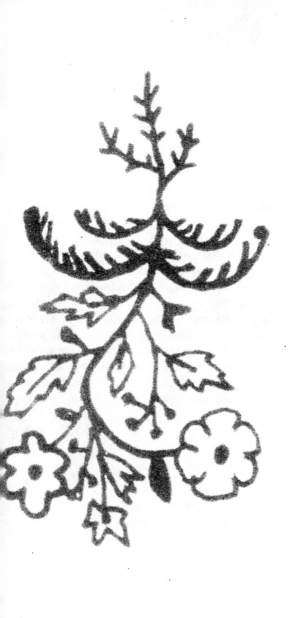

WRITINGS

IN TOLUCA HILLS
set an intention, establish voice

I am writing with something burning on my mind. The door is open, the radiator blows 74 degrees, and nothing is on fire—but something in my mind makes its way through my capillaries and exhausts itself through my fingertips. I am putting out the fire in the only way I know how.

In and age, where there is an increasing lack of clarity, I write. And why, will become clear for both of us.

describe your environment

-

I am writing from a second-story flat situated near the woods in an apartment complex known as Toluca Hills, and the door is open and the radiator blows. Outside there are oakwood trees, Moreton Bay figs, and jacarandas, though I cannot see the latter. We often write about what we cannot see, but I am not to write about purple trees. I am to be writing poetry, finishing up what has become a very ambiguous introduction to my literary work. The deadline was March 1st, then 7th, and now as April approaches, it could be any day I turn in my manuscript. This might get cut, but I hope it doesn't.

I'm in the company of a cocktail of herbs and spices and powdered mycelium and cacao. My sister tells me it is supposed to "open my heart." Angioplasty and an open window inside, fanning the flames.

23

continue

And outside there is noise from a not-so-distant highway and speedway motorists run red lights that I cannot see and outside there is news flying everywhere at a rate nobody can comprehend, which I cannot see. And outside there are millions of people afraid of catching something or giving something and who've convinced themselves that we better not shake hands. Even though we are family. Even though this is your son, we'd better wait until the whole world is vaccinated before you can be introduced as father.

In Toluca Hills, you don't get quaint coffee shops or happy hipsters—you get friendly jacarandas and neighbors named Bill and Susan and distant motorists breaking the law and you get space. You get a lot of space in Toluca Hills. You get 2400 square feet. You get two bedrooms and two and a half bathrooms. You get $3800 East Hollywood dollars for the price of $2400 dollars. At some point, there will be a complaint issued from the office for noise or a leaky vintage vehicle staining the lot down below. And you will not know where it comes from. Or who is reporting you. Yet the disciplinary protocol will remain the same.

If something is on fire, you better write or the place will burn down. And the fee will be considerable. Not to mention the paperwork.

evocation

I am writing as a full-time wide-eyed romantic clinging on to some increasingly vague ideal of what it means to be a man in America. Or anywhere. I am writing inside the complex. And outside there are cars and news and trees and none of them seem entirely sure about how things will play out.

apply contemporary concerns, use playful language

I don't mind the fact that the motorists speed up at the sign of a halt. It's as good of a guess as any when it seems increasingly evident that my peers are entirely lost to any sort of ideal. Increasingly more so, I find myself fulfilling the role as "cheerleader" to their passions. And I am increasingly terrified that my role seems somewhat futile and their passions aren't the main focus of my peers, but their lives having any meaning. Their ability to determine if at all, they are even real has become increasingly vague. I am even more terrified that more and more, it seems to me the only thing we may have in common. And yet, I feel totally estranged from the culture at large. I am entirely devoid of any satisfaction from the common dialogue. From the stories that make the page, from the conversation at hand. This past year there have been civil rights movements, capital insurgencies, and breakthroughs of what should seem like incredible "progress." Things we are told over and over that are "unprecedented."

In the past year from my observation, there has been nothing that has changed except the psyche of the mass. The increased individualism has reached the edge of the cliff and is starting to at best, parody itself. More accurately, it is eating itself.

Anthropophagus.   Angioplasticity. Alliteration. Patterns.

The idea that we are harbingers of change, of some radical movement is yet to be seen, and I am a romantic and I can't see it. Like the jacarandas and the motorists and the flying papers, I know they're there. But I can't see them from where I sit.

return to narrative voice, conclude

And I can't see them from the massive living room. Or from a bedroom that was fitted for my son. Or the other bedroom, outfitted for Gloria. I can't see, like they can't see...anything romantic about the current circumstance. I have cut myself off from social media and have become increasingly aware of how consumed I'd have been. And how consumed we all continue to be. And I find it despairingly evident that the crisis of the individual and fractured identities are par for social discourse. Nobody sees themselves as left or as right. The idea of a "normal life" has been driven so far off the map that anything close to nuclear is laughable. And I, in the midst of this, only want to laugh.

But I can't when the headlines and phone lines are all delivering the same message and nobody seems to be asking the appropriate questions.

I have a couple: What are we letting happen? Do we actually believe the things we promote online?

They have one: What are you going to do about it? For starters, I am getting off. And in time, I do believe that we all will. But in the meantime, the door is open and the window too. The radiator keeps things just temperate enough for a spontaneous fire to not break out. And I am contractually obliged to write a number of words and stories, and they came out at random as follows.

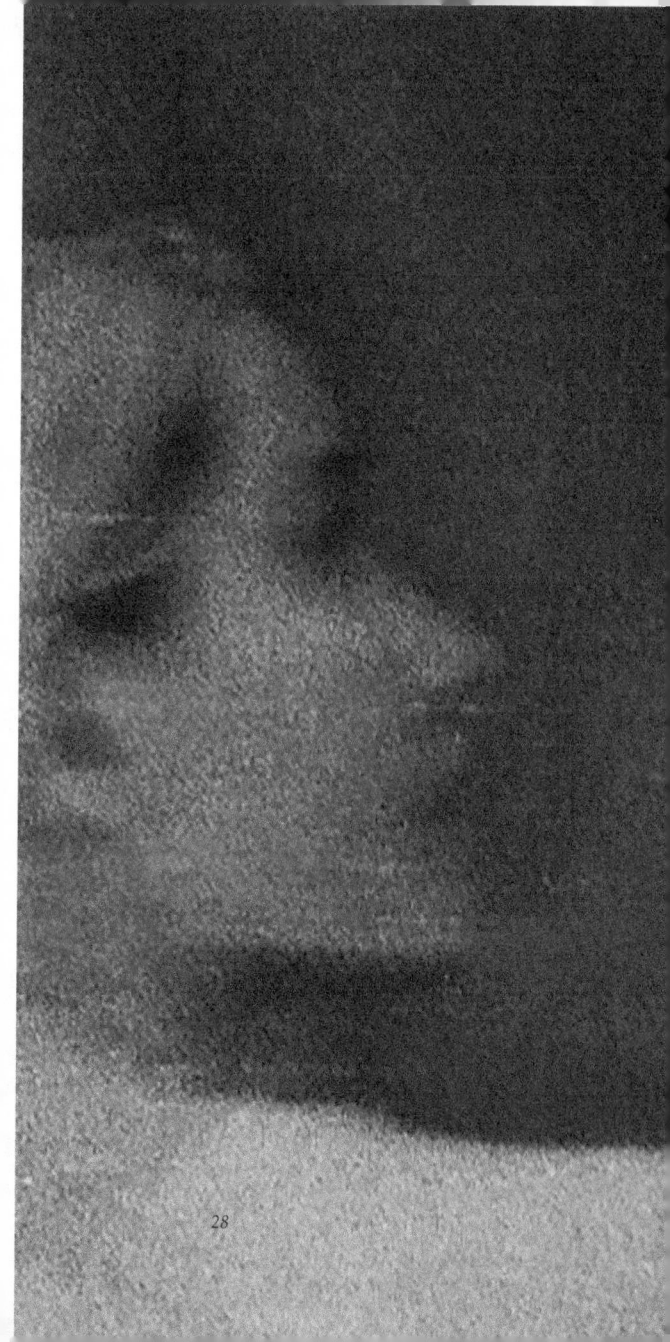

LIVE AND LET DYE

Every day I gaze at paradise.
I do not look for too long. I do not have to.
It's right there.

...

I consider that immediacy can be a numbing
agent if you aren't too careful. Stop looking, stop
working it out. Stop solving the problem. The
answer finds its way back to the white chalk, the
gunshot bang of the foot race. An invitation back
to yourself in the moment, these moments.
On your mark, get set...run like hell.

...

I always wondered if those were real bullets
coming out of the gun, and for that reason
have developed an uncontrollable and entirely
irrational fear of black-and-white striped men,
specifically the ones with guns pointed towards
the heavens. These folks are known formerly in
America as "referees," "umpires" or "officials."
They look away and pull the trigger towards
the heavens, taunting gods. All while dressed
like zebras or accountants who are also decent
and reliable husbands. What was their aim? I'm
captivated. Who wakes up, gets dressed, counts
backwards, never actually says "go"? Only to
blow artillery at the clouds? These folks.
Well-dressed and ill-mannered.
I wonder if these men—the ones who call the line
in organizational combat, at Olympic games—I
wonder if they wake up and look out windows.

...

I wonder if, in 1936 Berlin, Hitler gave strict instruction to his Stripes, demanding to call it in favor of the Krauts only to get their ass kicked by Jesse Owens, Black American. I bet he later shot the ref without considering even for a second how faithful or reliable of a husband he was. I wonder if Jesse liked it better in Nazi Germany than in the segregated and wildly black-and-white, 1930s America. I wonder what the appeal of that generation's furniture and decor is to my peers. Americans of the 1930s are referred to (officially) as the "Silent Generation." And unofficially as, "Radio Babies."

...

I find it quite appealing that right now, there is no furniture in my home. Although what makes it on the floor is a particularly confusing landscape. As follows in 10 pt Palatino font and italicized:

1. *Empty squirt bottles circa your grade school lunch hour*
2. *Solo cups circa your high school social hour*
3. *One comprehensive and illustrated guide to stretching*

...

Earlier, I'd gotten the itch in line at USPS and had to come back home for a page to scratch. To write immediately, to use the floor and its contents.

To myself, I announce: "I will be an Olympian for this stretch of my imagination. The bottles are to put colors on garments. And then to wear or sell. I am many things, yes, but today I am a professional tie-dyer (dyeist?). I'm not a postman or really anything. Today I dye all the beautiful garments of the world with dictatorial control and the discretion of a fifth-grader, the precision of a record-breaker."

And I will thank everyone I love from a screen and let them know that they are safe from harm. No one is to taunt their god today. Nobody is to compete to win the freedom of returning home. There shall be no one to judge the line or watch the clock. And no striped officials will yell at your face, just to tell them that they're "safe." This is official and I will announce "touchdown lovers!" without aggression. "You made it back from work. And even if you performed poorly, nobody took aim at your heart. Safe."

...

I always hated sports, but I always loved to stretch. All limbs and imaginations. I am a limber American, who (at times) proudly despises the place. I have an American boy who speaks perfect American French and he will grow up in a perfectly despicable American world, much different than mine.

My thoughts in 10 pt italicized Palatino:

1. *He may or may not have furniture.*
2. *Post offices may not exist.*
3. *Pot will still be legal.*
4. *Currency will not be green, but I hope the grass is.*

...

I'm writing in the living room where, as a result of recent technological advancements, the lights just turn themselves on. Typically at 5:00 PM, which is now, I can see exactly where my night will transpire.

I will extend my limbs and look in every Cardinal and peripheral direction. I will reach past every hemisphere and everything which splits the world into binaries. I will not expect anything.

...

As I become increasingly flexible, I will allow myself to be as I am and I will write to us. We, who may go entire work days racing in ovals for our dear lives, for our fellow countrymen. Proving to nobody we are Jesse Owens. We can do every thing. Every single one of 'em (things), But as for me, that itch won't ever scratch until I've turned the page black and I will turn and turn and only stop to spread myself out or to thank God I'm not a aren't a referee or a Nazi or an accountant. Or an athlete or a god getting shot at.

...

At the end of today, my hands will be stained. I will have applied fixative and soda ash and thiox to cotton in soaking hot water. I will observe as colors bleed, commune and wash away.

This vat of color will sing some solitary hue. Strict divisionary lines aren't really possible in the face of moving water. Nature will stitch you into it's fabric. And something less natural, may tell you you're better off on some team than staying naked. I'll toss and launder this fabric and smile. It looks like some strange uniform. And it's obvious enough to go unnoticed. I will wash my hands of the cloud killing umps, hang notions up to dry and I might laugh thinking, "Oh, it's shirts versus skins."

/PETROLEUM SERMON

When fuel explodes in a cylinder, the force of the explosion creates a reaction pushing the piston down. The motion of the piston causes the crankshaft to turn and ultimately propels the vehicle forward.

It isn't until you need to know these things that you do. And this is one of those moments. Dan lifts the hood on the side of the highway and says just enough for me to know it's bad. More precisely, he says nothing.

Dan, my mechanic, is somewhat of a myth around Los Angeles county. I've heard him referred to as a "guru," a "mystic," "that Mercedes guy out in Studio City." He is an expert on the Mercedes W123. Known informally as the "million-mile motor," these vehicles run off diesel fuel, maintenance, and a mystic guru mechanic. Dan knows all you could possibly know about keeping these vehicles alive for as long as sensible. We must've just hit a million miles before he told me the car had lost power, and slowly made our way to the side of the 134 heading west and just before the 5. A few moments later and we'd have made it to exit Buena Vista, Spanish for something more beautiful than "the side of the road."

I don't know Spanish very well. I don't know mechanics very well. I don't know much about pistons, other than that they are an essential component of the vehicle moving.

When it finally set in that the car wasn't moving without help from a Samaritan—professional or otherwise—I asked what had happened.

"A rod went through the engine."

It sounds pretty bad. It is. In fact, it's nearly the worst thing that could happen to a vehicle. And these things just happen. A metal rod that connects the piston to a crankshaft and moves you down the road piercing a hole through your engine is just something that happens.

And it happened to have happened just now.

If it happens when the piston is on its way up, it will be permanently jammed in the cylinder. If it happens on its way down, a connecting rod pierces a hole directly into the engine. In the field, this is what they call "throwing a rod."

Throwing a rod is terminal. There is nothing you can do for your engine after you "throw a rod." After that you try to remember the number for free California roadside assistance. After that you sit with your car mechanic, Dan, assessing his temperament and realizing this could take hours. After that, you surrender your day and wait for a Samaritan. It took twenty minutes. After that you are towed to a beautiful view. After that you are here at her final resting place.

It could've been anywhere. But it's here. At 439 Bob Hope Drive, bleeding black gold all over the road. With her back turned to the San Fernando Mountains, just past the Forest Lawn cemetery. Exsanguination underway. Dan goes to the corner of the park we've found ourselves in, presumably to mourn the loss. Presumably to phone a ride. I'm only certain of the latter.

As he hangs up, I offer my consolation.

"Of all the places for her to go, it isn't the worst place."

To my surprise, the consolation is taken and Dan agrees. He agrees because he isn't the type to mourn. After all, he's been doing this for longer than I've been alive, and this is the name of the game. In fact, just two days prior he'd picked up another "Merz." Some dialogue is exchanged about circles of life, karma, etc. These are the things you say when you have to.

I say my final words. "Well, my time with this one was short, but sweet." I snap a photo and the man on the other line to Dan arrives to take us back to the lot.

I only had the white one for two days, and I'm feeling a surprising amount of grief. Dan has had her for twenty years. It was his first one. The vehicle that started his million-mile preservation initiative. And now, she'll be picked up and escorted to some lot to become a "parts queen."

A "parts queen" is an industry term for old Mercedes who have run their course. These queens have inevitably suffered blood loss on their way to the pageant. Some of them were subject to poor maintenance. Some of them made it to a million. Most of them have not. And now they are parts queens: vehicles whose whole is now worth less than the sum of its parts.

In this business, the demand for parts is remarkably high. These parts are no longer manufactured. They are located in Alhambra, San Marino, San Diego, and innumerable other places across the globe where shipping is a financial liability.

Though these vehicles are known for their long lifespans, you are constantly swapping out parts big and small. One or two things go wrong, and you're scouring the terrain for a hood or a review mirror, a window, a button, or an engine whose guts are intact. If you're lucky enough, you know enough to know somebody who collects the old beauty queens.

Dan, owner of the now-deceased white 300sd, knows enough. In fact, he might know the most of anyone in Los Angeles county. I know this through observation. Just two days prior to us sitting on the side of the Ventura highway with a now defective vehicle, we had picked up a vehicle from Jim. Jim was a former marine. He lives in San Diego. Because Dan is fixing the vehicle I rent from his lot, and because I'm fascinated by these vehicles and the fight to keep them running, I offered to drive Dan.

Jim has had the light tan (once peach) vehicle that sat in his lot "since new." He should have never let it sit there.

Jim explained to me that NASA should have never abandoned the Apollo. He explained to me that because NASA abandoned manufacturing these crafts, we now have space trash in the atmosphere we will never be able to retrieve. Dead auto parts floating in outer regions of space to mingle with asteroid bits and signals from distant regions of space. Jim speaks of this as if it were the beginning of the end of America. He explains his aversion to helicopters and the invariable risk of ever getting into one.

"We just don't have the science to predict the wind," he explains. He would rather walk. Anywhere.

This conversation lasted all of ten minutes before Dan had confirmed that indeed, Jim's former peach was worthy of fixing up. The gentlemen made the exchange.

The conversation was as follows:

Jim: "I've taken her to every mechanic I know."

Me: "Well, Dan must be more than a mechanic."

Dan: "I know enough for it to be dangerous."

Jim: "Glad you're giving her life. I didn't want her to be a parts queen. I should have never let it sit there."

We laugh in the way that you do when you've all got other things to get to. I followed Dan back to his lot from San Diego to Burbank to make sure he got home without any incidents. Along the way, he phoned me to say we would make a pit stop in Anaheim for some parts, omitting specificity. He phoned me fifteen minutes later to say, "We better just head home. The brakes are going out."

Once you are an expert in the field of intuiting the overall stability of a w123, you make these calls. You sense the language of your vehicle and all its parts. And if the language is something you haven't learned, then things get lost in translation.

Money gets lost, parts go flying, engines get incisions. And all you must do is listen to know when to attend to your vessel.

I think back on Jim, the aviation enthusiast with the peach. I think of his aversion to helicopters. I think of space trash, of blood loss, of parts and models and queens.

I think of Forest Lawn and of beautiful views and the legal name, "Hope." I think of how all these cars, made of steel, will someday be long gone. We'll never be able to retrieve some things. Like the dead satellites mingling with extraterrestrials. I think of eulogizing Dan's first. It comes to me in the thundering of a piston as I turn the key and fuel explodes and pistons pump and shafts get cranked and I'm propelled forward.

This is one of those moments. It isn't until you need to know these things that you do. May we all make it to a million miles.

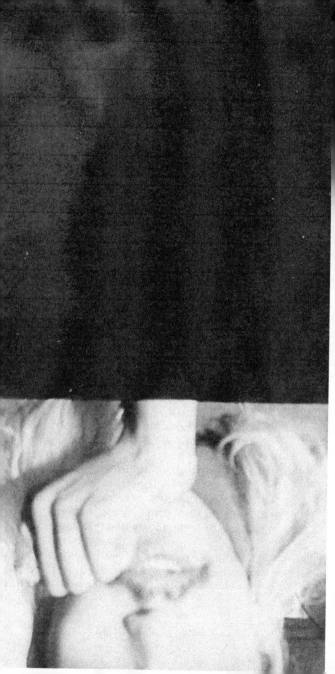

MARLBORO SUMMER
in three acts (of violence)

For the function telling this tale, I will pose a theory based on personal encounters.

Theory:
Being punched in the face can be a necessary component of becoming a well-functioning member of society.

Nothing quite humbles you like the altar you hold most dear being pummeled to a pulp. Just once. Once should be enough for most. Though there are exceptions to this notion. A notion only ridiculous only if you haven't had the daylight knocked out without warning.

Of all the humbling experiences one must encounter, this is in the top three. And while I'm not an expert on being a "well-functioning member of society" due to the arbitrary and subjective nature of this terminology, I can attest to acts of humility on behalf of Mother Nature.

Unsuspecting childbirth, calling off a wedding, getting cheated on, and getting punched. All great humiliators. Nothing else can let you know you have relatively little say in the width of your britches. I don't even know how to rank the lot in this hierarchy.

They're all tied.

I shall explain—and only from experience— three instances which I believe to have been inadvertently and painfully life-giving.

It took me nineteen years to get punched in the face. I can't believe it.

Perhaps I was unaware as to whether or not I had it coming. However, I did not once consider that it would come at all. And now, whatever is well-mannered and patient within me, any ounce of humility, can be directed towards in part, some generous fists.

ACT 1: THE CINCINATTI SALOON

It was the summer of 2010 and I had gotten punched in the face three times. Three times, in three different geographic areas, from three separate demographic groups.

It was the summer of 2010 and my head was held high. Outside of a dive in my hometown, the stage was set for the first of three acts in my story. This act was one of racial consideration. In fact, I was victim to what some might consider a hate crime. What most might.

Only shortly after stepping outside to light a cigarette, I'd been called a "Chinaman" from a neighboring group of strangers. Actually, the question had been posed as to whether or not I was a "Chinaman." Actually, it was about who the "Chinaman" was. I know now that they weren't really all that concerned with my race, but more so the fact that they hadn't been made my acquaintance.

Noticing that they were in the area typically assigned for smoking on nights such as these, and noticing that not a one of them had a cigarette, I made my way over to clarify their inquiry and offer up a peace pipe in the form of the Marlboro Man.

I was hit by a man adorned in camouflage.

Luckily for me, he was on heroin. Though I wasn't made aware of this fact until later, the punch did land in a particularly light fashion upon my ear. The impact was that of well...someone on heroin. And aside from a few seconds of ringing and blurred vision, little damage was incurred. I managed to maintain consciousness and stay upon my feet. Looking back, I'd like to consider this a warm-up for what would become an increasingly blistering summer.

...

When the police arrived, everyone was bloody. My brother's camera had been broken. And so too had my friend Kylor's lip. I remember when the policeman asked if I wanted to press charges, I said no. I was leaving for Chicago the following evening. I remember feeling that I had let Kylor down in some fashion taking into consideration that he had got the worst end of the deal. Yelling, "What the fuck? Is this the 1960s?" The cops drove off, failing to answer his question.

I didn't press charges for several reasons. One, I felt it would postpone my trip. And two, because justice need not be served to the man who laid the first blow. It had already happened. In the three seconds that I had lost my hearing, he had somehow ended up on the other side of the road, limp and with his blood spilling onto the sidewalk.

45

ACT 1: BOARDWALK

I made my way to Chicago, presumably for some business affairs regarding music. Presumably to do whatever you do when the only other alternative is the dive back home for the summer. In Chicago, you are worried less about getting punched than you are about getting shot.

Especially during the summer in point. It was 2010 and it was a historically violent summer. In fact, the saying goes, "Everybody dies in the summer." That saying can be attributed to Chancelor Bennet, Chicago native. This is well known. He is well known. And the song in which this declaration was made had just come out. The gangsters hibernate in the winter and come out of hiding in the heat, toting a piece and ready to claim their slice of pie in American headlines as the glorified capital of murder.

It never really seemed that dangerous ambling about Wicker Park, but if you turned on the radio or television you would almost certainly be informed that the body count was getting higher and higher. And the neighborhoods to which the violence was sectioned off had begun to spread their arms far and wide around the Windy City proper.

Nobody was safe. Daytime, nighttime, at home, or in hiding. But you can't stop living. Not in the summer of 2010 (fact check). And not on the Fourth of July when your best friend and brother come to town—this time, with a working camera. In my mind, we were entering some equivalent of the county fair. And the worst thing that could happen was a "Chinaman" getting blindsided while eating cotton candy.

We were late to the pier and caught only fifteen minutes or so of the fireworks before opting to walk a couple blocks further, looking for something, anything to fill the explosive blasts we'd missed. After all, we'd made it through city traffic to celebrate a day of independence.

As we walked, seventeen or so young black men (not a precise count) had been walking towards us from the opposite direction. The fireworks had just ended, and as the blasts dissipated, so too did the crowds. And the noise was coming from directions indistinguishable to my ears, one of which was already in questionable condition. One gentleman from the bunch, very young, broke from the crowd and began to divert towards my brother and I. I stopped dead in my tracks. I looked at the young man. He couldn't have been older than fifteen or sixteen. I knew exactly what he wanted.

A fresh, crisp Marlboro light.

I reached inside my breast pocket for a light and diverted my eyes only briefly as the gentleman proceeded light up my face. Like a smoke, lie a firework, like a fist to a face. Shouting came from all directions, and my eyes went blind for a few seconds. Feeling the grip of my older brother's arms around me, I could only make out a few statements. "What this nigga do to you?" "Fuck this nigga up!" And a familiar voice saying, "Just walk, man," as my brother, in superhero fashion, hoisted me upon his belly, leaving me no option to fight back—or at the very least inquire whether or not he indeed wanted to share a smoke and perhaps put an end to our differences, which were at the time incredibly vague.

To our great fortune, the melee had ended. As abruptly as it came. They walked away. That was it.

My brother let out a sincere inquiry: "What in the fuck just happened? Fuck this place."

I flashed back to Kylor's remark. There need/to be a reason in times like these. It needed to be tied to something. A civil rights movement. The increasing height of racial tension. But no. It was 2010 and it was very hot, even in the night.

And if race were the case, I wasn't sure who I was being made out to be—to which particular racial group I'd involuntarily signed up for as a militant representative. And I still don't know what I replied to my brother. And I still don't know about that cigarette.

ACT 3: THE REVELATOR

The third punch happened when I returned back to university in Bloomington, Indiana, a beautiful blue dot in a red state. If you were to get punched here, it would likely be by some drunken fraternity chap. It's likely it would not be a crime of race. It is unlikely that it would be you if you had been punched twice in the face just one month prior. And with only weeks in between.

It's even less likely that it would be from someone you adore and love and happen to be living with. Roommates, the colloquial term for people you live with. They are not on the list. But I had no list. And I found this sense of renewed optimism and outlook on life burgeoning. A remarkable side effect of a fist to the face.

In the backseat of my own vehicle, a Jeep Grand Cherokee with a sound system that had atrophied over the years, I sat behind the driver's side. And my roommate at the time, Kevin, behind the passenger. In between, Travis, fittingly the most neutral party in almost every situation that involved room and board or being mates. In the driver's seat, a sober and responsible friend shuttles us to where we all would go to lay our heads and drift into another intoxicating state of mind: sleep.

On the speakers was music. My memory is unclear as to what was being played. However, my general assumption is that it was my choice. A secondary assumption was to be made that Kevin vehemently hated the song as he began to punch the speaker, which already did not work. I told him to stop. Vulgarities were exchanged, and to my surprise they did not suffice.

I would like to interrupt this story to say this man I love dearly and he is happily married with children. At the time, he was unhappily divorced from a peace treaty in the form of a song less terrible. A song perhaps that Travis would have chosen. No slurs were exchanged. Only a couple of punches. A couple of punches so bad that my face looked like an onion, peeled and left out to embark on its journey through the spectrum of yellow purple.

After realizing that I had drawn blood, we had stopped. The technical terminology would be that I got my ass beat. Though I like to look at it as the third layer of my onion being revealed. I wore my face like a badge of honor. And in the morning, we'd apologized. Well, he apologized. And we shared a cigarette.

At no point did I consider this punch an act of racial discrimination. That is because it was not. At no point did I even consider it an act of malice. In fact, Kevin had not left his room for several days. He felt a level of guilt, I must admit was hard to dispute as my right eye barely let in any daylight. I couldn't justifiably tell him it was "no big deal" and look in the mirror at what looked like an uncut ruby: valuable, but not quite brilliant.

Looking in the mirror, I had to face myself. I had to face my face and the damage that had been done. Punches one and two had come close to allowing time for reflection. But the punch three was healing.

Before and over my very own eyes, I let it sink in.

I asked all of the appropriate questions any young
man who had escaped being punched in
the face for a very long amount of time. A young
man who has been punched in the face three
times in a very short amount of time.
What did I do?
Was it my fault?
Do I look like an asshole?
Am I an asshole?
Is this a karmic act? If so, am I finished being on
the receiving end? Is that how karma works?
No.
And the subcutaneous cells were regenerating
slowly over time. As my eyes grew wide and
my ego had narrowed, I thought that perhaps
the answer was more superficial. The questions
certainly were.
What if my eye never came back? And also, why
did two of the three punches come equipped
with racial epithets—racial epithets not typically
reserved for my race?
Admittedly, I had been called every name in
the book. But I had never been punched for that
reason. My mother is Filipino and my dad is
Croatian, and I at some point made peace with
the fact that by all accounts, I was whatever race I
was perceived as until clarified. By all accounts, I
was white...until I wasn't. Until I was told.
I certainly wasn't Filipino enough to claim that.
Not amongst my full-blooded relatives.
Maybe the punches had less to do with race, less
to do with even my face, and more to do with my
outlook. With the way I carried myself. Which
was, by all accounts, someone who had never
been humbled by brutal physical force.

You know the type of carrying I'm discussing. The kind that has little to no regard for anyone else in the room. And not in a wistful, free-spirited way, but in a way that Justin Bieber exemplifies to a T. Lauded by the culture and protected enough to be the rudest person on the face of a billboard.

Admittedly this is unfair to Mr. Bieber, and by all accounts, he may be an incredible gentleman. However, the image to which he has allowed for himself to be marketed as...that person does the carrying I'm talking about. I'm fairly certain that the real Justin Bieber carries himself with a bit more humility. I'm only slightly less certain that he has been punched if he does.

All relationships and wounds have been healed on my end, and I'm happy to say that I haven't been punched since. I'd like to believe that it is in part because I have learned through what hand-to-hand combat can teach. Well, hand-to-face exclusively in my case. I am aware now that physical violence is a reality. And while I don't cower in the face of reality, I also don't outwardly ignore the very real possibilities: the possibility that the man on heroin had a knife, or that the second punch could not have been prevented by my cavalier assumptions involving nicotine. I'm aware that my brother is not here to protect me, and that I had to learn how to do that on my own. And now for my own son.

Masculinity, as redefined as it seems to may be, is still rooted in a deep sense of humility. Outgrow your roots or your "britches," and someone may try to connect you back—to plant one right on the very place you hold dear. If I hadn't been punched then, I'm not sure when it would've happened.

And if I'm ever punched in the face, I've at least learned not to rely on the Marlboro Man or my brother to prevent it from happening. There are things you can't avoid. And learning this is just one of the many layers of the onion.

Know your onion. May it be consistently youthful and raw.

There are other metaphors for vegetables and couches to employ, but it may be better to lay it right on the face of this page. You can't avoid conflict. And there is a virtue in confrontation. Now that I'm a bit older, I can see past my eyes and my hands. And know that while you shouldn't seek it out, if you avoid it or are oblivious, the laws of nature provide for it to seek you out.

I know now which dives and piers to avoid, and at which hours. But it hasn't stopped this life from being one celebration of specific forms of independence. From the safekeeping of my brother's arms, from the luster of the city lights, from the merits and pitfalls of racial ambiguity and from the follies of young manhood. Life is beautiful. And it is one big holiday if you do so choose. There are fireworks and shots fired along the way, but in time you learn to catch them on time. I'm not going looking for my next big hit. I will take all the punches life will throw my way. In the form of breakups or shake-ups...or getting knocked on your ass, new life always appears. Brutal as it may be.

CHAPTER SEVEN/ BITS OF STAIN GLASS EVERYWHERE, ALL OVER AND I FEEL FINE

scattered lyrical fragments

/MOTHER SONG

Son you are a father now
Mama always showed you how
Selfless, helpless one could make
Make holy even your mistakes
Pray you'll stay a faithful man
And wash your sins and wash your hands
Apartments in the holy land
Holy water, ceiling fans
If you die, don't go to hell
Don't put faith in wishing wells
Fables that the gurus tell
I revere a great big book
But sometimes take a closer look
There's something 'bout what they don't tell
Bet Jesus tripped before he fell and
Probably ate the apple too
Found out what he'd already knew
I'm overdue if this is true
I wanna dance like I used to
I wanna live and be renewed

...

And as for you:
Just be yourself and don't you hide
I'll be there if you're crucified

/PILOT SONG

Anew with baby blue again

The doctor blew his brains

Sayin' Jesus H. Christ my boy

Forgot my middle name

The coroner was croonin'

In the corner with the swan

And they flew him to the tailor

As the pilot stitched along

**And a one two three four

Swimming through the swinging doors

She ain't nobodies mistress

It's just what she gets her kickin' for

Crash into the ocean at the condo tale vous

Pretty bitchin' in the kitchen

You explain your point of view

To the

Baby who is 8 or so

But 10 of 'em respond

It's a bird, it's a plane and the chemtrails are to blame

For the weeds

Crowding up the lovely lilies in my lawn

It's a bird a plane, but the heroes are to blame

For satellites and supermen

Who block my view of dawn

Talking bout the weather

Wearing boots of spanish leather

Said he did it all for kicks

But he did it all for heather

And Patti was a sinner

In the eye of the beholder

But his eye it was forsaken

In pursuit of rock n' rollers

And they cuff the kid who cop it

And they off the cops that stop it

And the doctor's all sewn up

But the needler had to drop it

It happens all the time
But too infrequent to be often
For us to lay this all to rest, all dressed
To paint our golden coffin

And now penny's playin' poker
With the pirate's one big eye
Just when things were lookin' up
He got killed for his supply

And penny loved the pleasure
And the pirate roamed the plain
For big forgotten treasures
Like Jesus' middle name
And sheila now is dancing
And the plane it rolls along
And everyone's a winner
And god knew it all along

And bobby was a lib

Brothers brains are on the lawn

Oh no! Jackie goes

The doctor! Where's he gone??

But the baby's all grown up now

And he calls the king a pawn

And all the wild horses

Who will sing a siren song

In the country with the princess

We go fishing for some truth but

Off with their heads, the fishes dead and in the
kissin' booth

A saint comes marching in

Patti prays upon the lawn

And a zeppelin crash

A lightning flash while he was on the john

And baby that was Elvis

And baby will be the king

Eating peanut butter sandwiches

With extra diamond rings

And the doctors resurrected

But everybody's gone

So he just drops the needle and the song plays

On and on

And all the wild horses in the sun

How am i supposed to get any writing done when Jesus' middle

Name is heather?

―――――――――――――――――――――――

*Clap your hands together in a 4/4 rhythm and finish one line per two claps.

Note: if you made it here before reading this, please go back and try again with

Friends or alone

**Shout this time

/SONG, SONG

Simple song

One song

Song, song

Writer's song

Songwriter's song

Song for the newly deceased

Song for your newborn

Newly released

Song for the blue

Moon song

Holy song

Psalm, psalm

Nondenominational

Non-condemnational

Congregational

Conversational

"When i sing song, you say

Sing"

"This is the part i wanted to show you"

Song

"This is the song i show you to love you"

Song

"This is the song i hear when i see you"

Song

This is the best song in the world

Self-referential

Song

It's talking about you, to you, for you, from you

Song

Song for friends

Song for funerals

Weed song

Long song

First song

Worst song

Best song

Your song, your song, your song

This song

"Wow i've heard this a million times, but it's
never sounded like

This

Song"

Theme song

Her song

Hymn song

goddddddddd (sforzando)

Song for Anthony, apple, father

Song for matriarch, mother, martyr

Song to bring you home

Song to take you there

There, there

Away, away

A way with words

Couple couplet's

Ain't ever heard

Song

Top of the pops

Top of the charts

One for the money

Two for the heart

Hearts of palm

Desert song

No-name song

Siren song

Woop,woop

"Nobody move, nobody gets hurt" song

"Nobody breathe, nobody gets choked" song

Swan song

Song for America

Son of Sam

Song for Elliott

Snow white song

Song for David

Song for Kurt Jr.

Song for those who couldn't hear the music

Song for nobody in the room

Song like nobody's listenin'

Song

Shoot for the song

Even if you miss you'll land upon a song

Song to lose it to

"An' a one, an' a two"

Song to remember

Song to forget

Song of triumphalist

Song of regret

Song of summer

Song of retreat

Song of reverence

Bow at the feet

Beat up and down, feelin' all damned

There's a song for renewal, revision

/(SUDDEN BEGOTTEN INTERVALES)

Really?
The whole way home somehow forgetting that
We   are
The   music
makers and
                    We

                              Are
The

                              Music
And if we
        See
              It
                    Is
        Possible
We need only to step into the podium and play
us a wand
And a 1,2,3, 4....

To the publisher-
Willie,
You've needed me to be a writer of poems, but
in earnest I have no idea what that means. I can
only assume some platitude, like "becoming
your discourse with the world." Tell me, do
you remember that one time you did something
seemingly devastating? That conversation you
had that provided equal amounts of terror
and peace? The venturing into this inferno...
well that is not the job of a poet, but the job of
a human. A poet may just be someone foolish
enough to take on the role as translator.

Best,
Joseph

SILVERBELL
CITY
POEMS

A few more Eiffel towers and l think this place has really got what it takes to be the next Paris

/Hollywood Poems
3, 6, 9, 0 and More

3

Madonna

Beck

Mac Demarco

Moby

Tom Hanks

Nick Cave

Taylor Swift

Ariel Pink

These are the people I know

She says

You recognize some of these names

You do not recognize others

It means nothing

6

She says

Knowingly

That she knows

Lots of other people

And what's more

They all have names

And they made them

She says

For themselves

-

9

Nothing

Which is who you are

If you do not know these people

She says also

And you begin to think of lifting weights

But leave them there

0

You tell your friends

Who say, with conviction

It's nothing

Your name

If you do not know these people

Only they don't know

You've known secretly

Your name has never really meant a thing

More

And you buy a cheeseburger

And you see a billboard

And you see names

And you start to see something

And it terrifies you

You play guitar to calm down

It's a good one

She says

In lights

She can see my name

There are visionaries

And they are everywhere,

Here

My Neighbor #2

My neighbor bill, he knows my name
And where I live
And stay indoors
At least
For months he's wondered
Is he alive
And for months
Me too

My Neighbor #3

Bill, the daywalker
Neighbor emeritus
And tenant to the complex
He surveys the land
And will greet you
If you are so lucky
Saying
I heard about the car and the kid and the keys
and all that
I'm sorry they all run away
I don't know how you do it
Run away?
You say
He says
No - you stay
And I don't know either
Yet I'm certain, as bill confirms
That the weather, it sure is nice today

...

This exchange
Over a glance and a top heavy side smile, saying
"you alright?"
And I am now
With a neighbor like you

Sonnet for ending discrimination

Perpetually discriminating, justifiably
discussing reality
Justifying perpetually discussing
discriminatory reality
Really discussing a justifiably discriminating
reality
Discriminating justifiably, discussing reality
perpetually
Perpetuating reality, discriminating discussion
justifiably
Really justifying discrimination, discussing
perpetually
Perpetual reality rarely justifiable,
discriminating discussion
Really perpetuating discrimination, rarely
justifying discussion
Discussing perpetual discrimination, justifying
reality
Discriminating reality, discussing perpetually
justifying
Rarely a justice discussion, perpetuating
discrimination
Discriminate perpetuating justifying reality,
discussing rarely
Rarely discussing really justice, discriminating
reality
Really rarely discussing anything, perpetuating
discrimination
End discrimination by perpetuating a living
discussion in reality!

LOVE IS AN INVITATION ON FIRE
A LETTER
TOWARDS THE PEACEFUL MAN
IN HIS PEACEFUL HOME AT PEACE WITH
HIS PEACEFUL WORLD
ON FIRE

I SAT WITH MY FIRE BY MOONLIGHT IN HIDING
THROUGH FIG TREES AND HEAT. AND IN
SICKNESS AND IN HEALTH I'VE HELD OUT MY
PALM TO THE HOLY SPIRIT WHILE FLAMES LAP
LIKE CANINE COYOTES - ALSO PRESENT - AND
ONE LAUGHING AT THE SUPPOSED WEIGHT OF
THE TALE I TELL MY LIFE. AND ME LAUGHING
TOO ON A GOOD DAY. AND ON A GOOD NIGHT,
I SAT WITH MY FIRE.

I write to the Patron Saint of Percussion

"AND BY FALL, WE WON'T
AND BY THIS TIME NEXT YEAR OUR BOYS WILL
PLAY IN THE YARD AS WE BUILD US A SHED
AND BY DINNER TIME, WE WILL RUN BACK TO
OURSELVES. HAPPY SUNDAY."

Becoming a member of society

Fiercely believe in a bigger thing
Adopt a sense of universality
Draw that to its logical conclusion
Accept that you will be wrong
Admit that you are nothing

Compile an empire of esoteric text
Write out loud
Lose your mind
And your paper
Do research to get high
Accept that you will be low
Adopt new association to money
Establish metrics to valuate value
Develop a highly concrete notion about your self
Wear that suit - exterior
Abandon your notion about yourself
Be naked - interior
Remember you will die
Hardwire brain
Feel joy
Notice things
Notice all the things
Notice how noticing makes you feel, do away with
noticing that

Develop a dialogue with the things you create
Remember you will die
And that is why
You
Put out the art already
Make new art

Make two new art(s)
Burn one at random
Frame the other and place it in the center of your living room
Do not sell this piece
Make one more art
Give it to your mother
Give up
Fall in love with another mind
Make a child
Abandon all prior notions
Learn to unlearn
Re-learn everything
Fall in love with another mind
Lose yourself in that person
Fall out of love
Remember you will die
And that is why
Learn from your child
Notice him noticing you

Remember you were born
And that is why

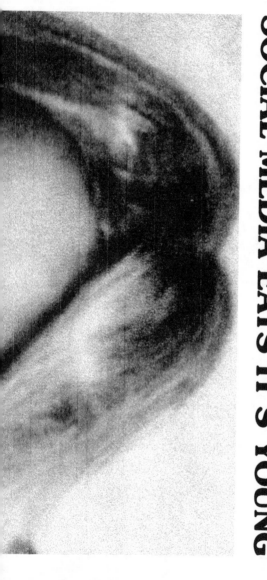

SOCIAL MEDIA EATS IT'S YOUNG

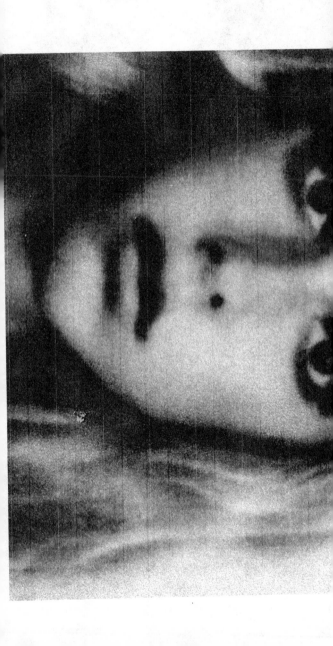

Dear Boy

I have been here every day. And though I don't
outwardly show it, I've reached a previously
incomprehensible amount of pain. The pain
which does not cease, even in my sleep where
quite often I dream of you. Last night I'd a dream
you were of legal driving age, going fast. And
I woke up in a fever manner, reaching for the
keys. I am terrified that my heart may fail me.
I have no refuge, even in my friends. It is not
unlikely that I ruin someones night, by allowing
myself to be fully honest about being forced into
silence. And so, even amongst my dearest of
friends - there is no withdrawal from the pain of
your absence. The pain which is second only to
the love that you have filled me with. Before you
were born, I'd asked a close friend "Do I have
what it takes? I'm entirely too emotional for all
that's to come." They re-assuredly said, "You-
if anyone, has the capacity." And now, these
friends have grown more and more deficient
in their ability to relate. If I find a punctuated
moment of joy, it feels fraudulent - a pale
imitation of my moments with you. In some very
strange way, I feel that only you know this pain.
I see in your eyes, that you feel it too.

...

Your grandfather, the doctor- he has healed wounds of old. Yet, even he could not prescribe or diagnose my pain away. It is my pain exclusively. In time, you will see the inexplicable terrain of this country, this city. Do not let a single soul trick you not to feel. Or tell you there is even a spectrum to live within. You are color unbound. And to behold all that is foreign to the shortsighted eyes of Hollywood.

There is nobody to blame, but there is a wicked teacher named fear. And it consumes the richest spirits. And in my short time as a father, I've known only to turn and kiss fear on the mouth. It is a laughable force in the will you've inherited. And you will meet your roots. And as you grow, you will realize the weary limbs we inherit. And the sometimes fickle mind, that gives way to immediate pleasure. Your father's father is one whose sins have been forgiven. And despite any transgression I've held, I see him as nothing less than an entirely and perfectly flawed human. As I see myself and have grown to understand. But you, my son. You are pure. And you will always maintain this purity. I will get this printed. They'll make a thousand. And you will have permanent reminders unbound. Outside of covers and shelves. The greatest technology is a language unspoken. You speak it to me. You have since we met. And far before, we met on this impermanent plane.

There is no unknown tongue to the child. It is in all of us, kicking the door down, and into this world to be entirely embraced by the mother of this good, green soil. Unleashed into some massive thunder-lily rain forest where all the children and good gods disguised as flowers and lizards play. Something within you, will force it's way out. And you may mistake it, if you believe what small minds impose. But no-it is you, it is you as you are now, wearing your inner child on your sleeve indefinitely.

For too long, I've longed to teach you. And to be taught. And that's our deal, okay?

And all I feel I've been unable to proclaim - it will make it to you through the page. Of this, I am certain. I could die today if it meant peace in this life for you. And I would leave behind a trail, a legend, a compass and reference material.

93

Encyclopedias, thesaurus, dictionaries, all the
dead sea scrolls and artifacts with language no
living linguists could ever pronounce. It is our
code. It is all in here. Just look with one loving
beautiful eye. Do not squint. Do not try. You
have only to cease any effort to see. All of it.
Close your eyes and experience me, your father
who loves you very much. Who is flawed like his
and in time, you will know that this is alright. In
fact, this may be the way. Break through. Carry
yourself like the pieta, sacred and marble mother
and son. It is all within you. Just turn and face
the pain and watch it dissolve. This is a super
power. The peace I've maintained has come only
through mysteries. In the face of terror, cast
fear back into it's cave. Where there is no light
to create the illusion. These seemingly powerful
tricksters are laughable in the face of love.

I know you must know, you must. But why am I
being forbidden the joy? Why are you? And how
could anyone identify a father's love as anything
less than mandatory? It is not your fault or mine
or the fault of social hierarchy and status. It is
not the fault of anyone who falls prey to fear. It is
an unfortunate truth that we're being sold fear. It
keeps big minds in small spaces. It keeps voices
meant to sing loudly, from speaking at all. It
destroys communities and it stifles art.

From birth you've known this. And at birth you
are fearless. Remain uninfluenced by those at
the mercy of fear. Stand tall amidst the pressure
to feel or believe you are anything less than a
singular and perfect soul. You will see these
things. You will.

You will notice everything. And though it may feel at times, like it is all too much, it is never not. And that is just enough. Little by little the world will reveal itself. And it needs you, like I need you.

There are lessons learned in all of the minute details of the day and in the drifting and sometimes sleepless nights, may you have an immovable peace and knowingness.

I'd my life shattered time and again. And I'm still here. And if it would've been easy I would not have cared.

Touch the world with your mind. And make no effort, in doing so. You will become all that you are. And someday we may look together at this text unfold, writing it together with our eyes. And we will know. And we will laugh. Finally and together. You see the inexplicable and entirely familiar details. There is a poet William Blake and he saw the world in a grain of sand and there is a poet Saint Therese who saw the world in a little flower and there is a poet little Indigo who sees the world. The world sees itself in you. You are.

/Notes from Sunset and Magnolia

w/ Gloria
I talked to two mystics today.
The first was a coffee maker who
Offered generously, "writing comes when I'm not
writing...just listening."
I too - must contend that 90% of
writing has not to do with the act itself.
And together we wrote an epic over the pour alone.
-
The second mystic told me what happens when "love
happens,."
I could hear in their voice, an sincere
acknowledgment, saying "now that it's here, it's here
forever. It's not going anywhere." It is an important
message for me, in my current circumstance.
Waiting for the love of my life to be born.
And for the love I've always known- to return.
I thanked my brother and hung up the phone.

w/ Ramona
I'm finding it all around bullshit
What we tell ourselves and most of what we
hear. The real pulp of the peach tree is in the
silence, in that confident
voice inside that knows more than we could
ever. Hey genius, be good. Also-how good does
it feel to be alive? Sometimes the worst, but we
get it all and this song makes me weep and i
hope you had a lovely day and a lovelier night
What's this whole thing for anyway?

w/ Kansas
slowly and alone if at all and wow......Mallarmé
and all these old 19th century frenchmen...
we're chumming it up like we're playing chess
in washington square park

again
Mind blowing and a song and a song that is
playing always remembering to cherish this
fast life by moving at the speed of a friend in a
forever reincarnation you met as a tortoise in the
desert
-i have to show you nishnabotna and two-way
loving next time you're here
-niobrara and nishabotna...certainly the names
of some great wunderkids yet unborn

w/ Julia
really -
but i know enough to know that knowing is
enough and someone said that and for tonight,
it was me. Sleep well on platitudes and pillows,
longitudes that are temperate from north to
south

w/ Joan
The day was warm and beautiful and bright
and the sunshine too and now they get tucked
into the soil - we get to dawn and to wear the
evening of some spring and summer at the hand
of mother nature, the french designer

w/ Mom
sweet dreams
of natural light and pictures that take
themselves, take good care of you

w/ Andy
the positively strangest phenomenon has
been birthed out of this. every night, around
midnight to three , i awaken full of
creative energy i'd likely sought out earlier in
the day...and curiously to no avail.
theta brain waves wash over me with chatter i'd
surely missed amongst the weekly people day-
parade. d'ya know what I mean?

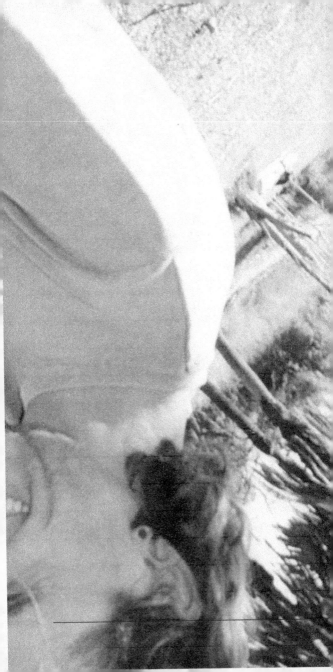

w/ Rhys
The shakespearean part of the whole cosmic
giggle is that no matter how well you can
anticipate the future, there are still extraneous
variables that will not allow for us to control
outcomes. We have can live in a state of
conversational surprise. I mean, that's gotta be
one of the richest and most playful elements of
the human experience...experiment? good night
good man

w/ Jackson
Either i'm stark raving mad
Or i'm stark raving mad and it's real
And it's almost too much only it is exact.
Tomorrow i am going to buy a box cutter.
I'm looking to my favorites dead guys who are
not dead-for inspiration. Have you been to the
DIY Hardware store around this way?

/SCENES FROM FLIGHT 24 TO GLORIA

SCENE 1: "Frictions and Premonitions"
There's a body capitalizing on the empty middle
seat
Setting boundaries and maximizing leg room
There's a woman walking with the same center of
gravity as a newborn
She's about to kick your foot
And offer an insincere and knee jerk apology
And yes, she does, she did
The encounters up here are all low impact

...

SCENE 2: "A Man Aboard"
There's a man in the back
A sick, sad angry man who is drinking the 787
dry
Overgrown and campaigning for support from
neighboring passengers
Nobody knows what "happened" or why he's
so angry, but he is loud and because of this,
people assume he's correct.
"Fuck you! Fuck you! Fuck you!" His slogan, is
painting the air we will all contribute to and fro
during our tin can exchange.

...

SCENE 3:"I am a Passenger"

Meanwhile. I'm trying to write you a sincere
poem about love, lore and tribulations
I need to write about old friends
getting married. Not getting invites to family
affairs. Missing the ones i am requested to...you
know, all the important and melancholic
sentiments you've come to expect.. I need to pull the
beauty from the overhead and overheard.
But all i get are vulgarities in frat boy rhetoric and rosy
cheeks from those too timid to speak up

...

SCENE 4: "Hark! Sing the Airborne Horns, Bellybutton Suite"

And alas turbulence!
The giant domino symphony of the belt buckle
panic from left to right and from coach to first
class. Nobody is feeling quite as bold as they
were when they unclamped and let it all hang out

...

SCENE 5: "Dramamine Transmissions"

*Hello strangers - this is your captain reminding you,
we're about to test fate and never see each other again.
Please watch out for any incoming aircraft as I take a
big nap. Welcome to Tin can Airlines. Where we all
somehow sleep and pray the ocean ain't hungry for
a geometrical...you know, uh...the bermuda triangle.
Good nigh or whatever!*

...

...

SCENE 6: "Anti-Social Hour at the Signal Mixer"
There's a snore that's overcoming timidity from
opportunist seat sleeper in 24b
There's a couple in front.
It's been six hours and i can't tell if they're
arguing or not.
Some say that's an italian thing.
I say it's just a thing.
They're definitely married though.
And actually i do think they are italian.
And they get close and smile and they look
offended and pull away and yell things for the
ether to pick up. Non sequitur words sneak into
the cargo air - out of place and out of context.
Words like "sleep" and "exactly."
Christ give me death before division
Ok good they're making out
I think they're fine

SCENE 7: " *Paul Rudd and Warm Blankets*"
There's the hum of the 100 some people who took
the initiative to go ahead and turn on their air
It breathes in tandem with the engine turbines
confidently barelling through turbulence.
The sleeptalking pilot annoounces that we're just
as safe here as in our living room. There's a blue
aura from atop the carry on section.
Green lights
Blue lights
And about 500 tvs
Almost all of them playing a 3d live update of the
flight status
Or paul rudd, american xanax
3.00 Twix king size candy bars

...

SCENE 8: "*Carry on*"
I'm barreling through the sky to the place you
lived for a million years
Where you misplaced your innocence and laid
waste to any idea of youth
This is your town any way you cut it
And i wish you were here
With me
Okay with just being anybody together
Watching the sun dance and the hungry ocean
Cheating death and landing just before mealtime

PLAY

The poet, the shrink

Setting: a shrink's office
Instructions: 1. Read as if you know who is speaking
2. Do not know who is speaking.

Hey poet
Hey shrink
Hey shrink i was thinking ya know...
How ya doin poet
Good and
I'm a poet y'know and...
What do you see when you look at this thing poet
Ok so —let's imagine your corpus callosum is
severed and you're free temporarily to make
Any number of wild
Associations
With as many accurate assessments of inaccurate
probabilities
I could say that a rose is as much a symbol of war
as it is for life, for love
I could say it tastes cherry and breathes like a
decent harvest
 I could use numbers
7, 13, 4 Million seventy seven yeses and 3.14
Infinities, 6, 15, 11..
Endlessly exploring every vista
All that could ever be not ever there always
—- Et al
And now

Imagine i could tie the knot back together
That ball and chain of binary thought
Of haves and wants
Of hemispherical junctioning
Any determinant factor
With which to arbitrarily place
Any limitation to experience

Ever
The superpower to jump back into the world of
linearity and association and give you a
straight answer and then
I see the rose you want me to
A rose is a rose and dammit don't we know
But we also know a rose is everything else now
too
Ain't it just
And why we're not talking about that i don't
know
But it's there
I know it's there
It's the reason i'm in this chair
Ain't it
The reason
They all stare
I can inhabit both worlds and am not committed
to choose
By habituation
No sir
Or socialization
No thanks
Or natural selection
Some national notion
Some nasally nation sticking its nose where it
don't belong

In my cranium
No
I'm not left to choose
I don't have to
You seem to have made my mind up for me
So i'm in your world doc
Yes i'm in your world
Concrete and mortar shells
Combines and motor skills
And motor cars
And cycled news
And no new beginnings
Yeah i'm in it alright
I'm in the game
I'm in the game
As much as you're in the game
But i didn't set it up
We know the rules, we play the rules
And we break them every time we let ourselves
play best friend to ourself
And play, play, capital p
I'll go along with your pharmacological almanacs
and affect side effect sideways thinking
Correct. I will play the game
But you know the gig is up
And the decks been stacked against you
As much me
We make a check work, check mate, rent freeze,
eat death and taxes
Not me no not now not on
We can't be beats
All dead anyway and happily
Anyone who knows already knows
And they're all right here
In this very room

Dancing all at once
Stumbling over your pedigree
Happily
And handing you a rose colored life doc
A victory dance it is
And i'll take you and embrace you
And we'll dive vast into the all nothing
The prerequisite to our birth
Was an agreement
To allow for something
As divine as this
To be possible
And how much we believe that
Is the game
What are you writing down?
Everything you just said
Put it in your book and call it "baba"
Call me in three months
And for the record, i am high as a kite and have
no idea what you just said
Please let the next patient in.

/Twenty Three

I was born right on time.

Late, but right on the time.

October 22nd 11:00 est 1990.

Twenty three zero zero. That's how it looks when you spell it out in military time. Using Palatino font.

Because of the scalpel like precision by the hands of fate. I came to be in eternity. Which is a great place to be born.

Thirty minutes later and i would have been a scorpion, not a scale. The scales beckon me to weigh and estimate all prophecies.

And so too, i can predict the very terrible future of a futile life of online chess, which i will later unpack.

The year 1990 was quite possibly the best year to be born in eternity town and on time.

I was a cognizant being before the desktop hellfire came home to all for mass brainwashing. I have a foot in the door of both worlds and based off of my studies, deem 1996 was the cutoff. We should not have gone past instant messenger. Or dial up.

Or

Landlines.

In any case, here we are.

Ah yes, and if my mother was not in labor for 40+ hours and pressured into cesarean, she would not have prayed to saint baba.

I would not have pulled off that miracle where I did a triple axel in her stomach. My name would not be my name. And i

Would not have heard the story with attribution to capital g, god. The catholic upbringing i had... Specifically in regards to fear

Lead me to examine death and spiritual intercession far earlier than i would have liked and so... This would not have been.

It was the best time. Being born.

/Interview

with the author conducted by Jack cardigan of the
Royal Philanthropic

Music:

I remember my father would do this. 4 Am.
Rocketing towards his daily routine, which consisted
of an innumerable amount of push ups and sit ups
and equals amounts of gasping breaths - which
mother must have found relaxing enough to sleep
through over the years of tossing and turning and
changing the sheets - and likely her mind.

Both of them would snore and occasionally sound
like some dueling instrumentalists some contest of
brass and woodwind proportion. My father taking
the lead as they grew into one organism and the
night went on. It was no contest. It was concerto.
It was union. This conclusion - the only thing that
allowed me peace as I too - tuned out the snoring and
crooned along - Sleeping loud and happy and safe.

Writing this book:

It was very painful. It was very pleasant. I wrote
most of it in Toluca Lake.

On Toluca Lake:

Great. Makes less of itself than east Los Angeles.
Frank Sinatra lived here. And there's a great
street name down the road - W.C. Fields Drive.

On poetry:

I had an idea of what poetry was. And now I have a different idea. Some of these ideas are in this book.

On reading this book:

Anyway you like.

On society:

We are all well aware, I hope...of how social media breeds mental instability and poor self-esteem. As a member of society, I propose we-redo the whole thing. Or abandon it entirely.

On shooting oneself in the foot:

I tried that. I would rather be shoeless than to walk the path of the less curious. - Bob Dylan said T.S. Eliot said Abe Lincoln said that.

On curiousity:

It is your direct link to immortality.

On grand statements:

Make them.
If you believe in them, make them. And do not explain yourself.

On love:

One drug you must take. And it will kill you. And it will redeem you. And that is alright.

On art being for sale:

It should not, but it is...And "everything is free" by gillian welch and thank you for engaging in the transaction required to hold this book.

On social media:

Death to sincerity and bad for art. And by that i mean a connection to the world, the community and your soul...

On community:

It is a vocation of mine to advocate for community gatherings of the most invigorating nature. It will be the only thing that saves us...Community (and nature).

On nature:

We should really pay attention to it.

On the world ending:

It is not. Not anymore than it was. And not anymore than it is.

On a world without community:

The end of the world. I believe however, we've it in us to speak up and embrace the things we don't understand.

On meditation:

Very advanced technology.

On living and dying:

Non negotiable and highly suggested. Embracing dying before you do might eliminate the fear...Of things actually being okay the way they are.

On the left:

Silly.

On the right:

Silly.

On politics:

Propaganda.

On American politics:

The most idealistic and novel constitutions unravel in the least ideal ways and are written about in novels which are then burned if they're good.

On the news:

There's a saying, "nothin' on the news, but the blues." Perhaps it is more accurate to simply state "nothin' on the news." There is nothing on the news.

On when Bob passes:

I will be very, very sad. And i will not let you know about it on social media.

On social media obituaries:

I hope they're sincere. But you know, they all couldn't be.
Oh yeah, and just very fucking weird.

On when I die:

Sing karaoke and see if i start to move.

On when I die cont'd:

I hope i go out singing and moving.

On moving along:

That's right.

RIGHT ON TIME
OUT OF NOWHERE
LEFT OF CENTER
TOP OF THE MORNING
BOTTOM OF THE NINTH
OUT OF THE PARK
INTO THE GUILLOTINE
OFF WITH YOUR HEAD
ON WITH THE SHOW
BREAK UP THE PAGE
END RIGHT ON TIME

WITH GRATITUDE -

LITA AND HENRY, MA AND PA AND LEONCIO AND DONATA MARY AND HENRY SR. AND HENRY JOHN WILLIAM CRANE KANSAS BOWLING JASPER MCMAHON ROGER STEFFENS AND MARY NAROPA UNIVERSITY ERNIE PYLE ALENA JASMINE BRITT COLE HENRY AGENT SMITH SMITH NUG GLORIA AUSTIN CHRISTINE PARKER JENNA JOHN JIM JAMES BO KOSTER ANNE WALDMAN FRANK VAHAN MERCEDES DAN SAM A. ELEISHA ANDRÉS V. RHYS DETROW JD AMBROSE BYE ERIC HOEGEMEYER JULES ALEX WINKLER Q KEV AND THE FOLKS BACK HOME TT THERESA MATICK JEREMY JOHN AGAIN MARIA JESS AND PASTY AND MELISSA AND BRANDON AND JOHN AND ERICA AND THE GREAT STATE OF INDIANA AND DAN AND DEBBIE WINKLER MERIJOY D AND ALL MY SIBS AGAIN MICHELLE AND DAN BEACHY QUICK JAYNA AND TONI OSWALD AND RIMBAUD LEE HAZELWOOD KURT AND ELLIOTT AND CRAIG N. JASON P. YOKO THE CLEAN BOBBIE GENTRY SCHMILLSON THE KIDS OF THE LANGLEY SCHOOL GARTH HUDSON KAMASI CHAPPELLE NIGEL YASIM TALIB ANDRE BENJAMIN SYD ADELINE JIMI KACEY SZA GIL SCOTT HERON C.W. SLY JOEY M. TREV AND HANY AND THE WHOLE SUNDAY BAND AND ALL OF LOS ANGELES FOR THAT MATTER THANK YOU TO ALL THE VENUES AND EVERYONE WHO HAS BELIEVED IN MY SILLY DREAMS I TAKE VERY SERIOUSLY JUSTIN MORAN ANTWUAN AND ANYONE WHO ENDS UP WRITING ABOUT THIS MATT G. IRA AND CICI AND ALL THE MEMBERS OF ALL MY BANDS AND MARSHALL AND ALL THE PEOPLE WHO HELPED ME THROUGH HARD TIMES EVAN AND SCOTTISH FRANKIE EVEN THOUGH YOU THOUGHT I WAS TOO AMBITIOUS AND WE PARTED WAYS ALICIA FEOM THE YORK MANOR ALL THE CHICAGO KIDS AND JULIE RAGOLIA AND EMILY AND LEX AND ENRIQUE AND MARCUS AND EVERYONE WHO HAS TAKEN CARE OF ME PROFESSIONALLY FRANKIE AND ROB FORD RIP I STILL PLAY PIANO AND MARY AND DAVE AND KIANI DON AND PITT AND SPENCER ANS HAILEY AND GABE MAC FROM BACK WHEN WE HAD A RECORD DEAL AND SEAN AND MARÍA AND CONOR FROM THE LIVE SESSION AND LUCA AND ANTHONY MY COUSIN AND GABE MARGUERITE TRAVIS AND KEV KBROWN AND ALL MY COLLEGE TEACHERS MR PETER JACOBI REST IN PEACE I LOVE YOU SARAH HARRIS AND ALL OF THE PERFORMERS ON SUNDAY NIGHTS HANNAH XUAN AND DAVY CLARKE JEFFREY LUKE AND LAEL AND STEPHANIE JANE ASHLEE AND NICK H. GUY AND SARAH FRANCESCA AND THE WHOLE FAMILY AND EVERYONE I MISS AND EVERYONE I MISSED AND BOB KAUFMAN AND JACK MICHELINE AND JACK AND RILKE AND MARSHALL M. W.B. E.E. D.H. T.S. LENNY BRUCE AND BOB DYLAN YOU WILL LIVE FOREVER CHARLIE PARKER MILES AND ALLEN JULIA C. BERNADETTE MAYER NICK BAKER AND CORITA KENT AND NORMAN LALIBERTE AND ALL THE BANDS I'VE PLAYED WITH AND NOT AND JON AND THE MEMBERS OF TMB GRIFF JOYCE WILLIAM STEIG JOSEPH PINTAURO NOEL LIAM MALLARMÉ AND STORIES AND SKYLIGHT AND FERLINGHETTI AND FOR THE ONES WHO TAUGHT ME TO PAINT AND THE ONES WHO SHOWED ME TO SEW AND THE ONES WHO TAUGHT ME POETRY AND THURSTON AND JOHNATHAN AND EVERYONE WHO WAS NOT MENTIONED WHO KNOWS AND TO ANYONE WHO WAS NOT MENTIONED AND QUESTIONS SURELY YOU UNDERSTAND BIL AND VIC AND FRANCIS AND CHRISTIAN AND SHARON AND JULIAN HARMON AND CONNOR TILLEY AND BETH AND ANNIE AND ANNA AND PHIRA AND ALL THE PHOTOGRAPHERS AND LAUREN AND LAURYN AND THE STATE OF TEXAS AND EVERYONE WHO THINKS I'VE LOST TOUCH AND D.A PENNEBAKER AND ALL MY AUNTS AND UNCLES AND ONCE AGAIN ALL MY SIBLINGS THERE ARE NINE OF YOU AND THATS WILD AND THERESA AGAIN FOREVER FOR THE DOCTOR AND THE PATIENT AND THE IMPATIENT WHO HURRIED ME ALONG AND HELPED ME ALONG THE WAY AND ALL THE STOCKISTS AND TO PHILIP L. AND TO COACH AND THE PEOPLE WHO PAID ME AND HEDI AND EVERYONE WILLING TO OFFEND AND LISTEN AND EVERYONE WHO WAS ABLE TO GET OFFENDED AND LISTEN AND TO COMMON GROUND AND EVERYONE WHO DID AND DIDN'T ATTEND ON SUNDAYS AND JACKSON ROSENBOBO OJ WOODY DARREN TO MY FATHER AND TO MY SON AND EVERYONE WHO ENCOURAGED ME TO WRITE A BOOK AND AGAIN TO MY TEACHERS AND AGAIN TO MY SON

THE BOOK ON WHY:

I'M WRITING ON BEHALF OF EMOTIONAL
VOLATISM AND ISOLATION AND ROUTINE
AND MIND GAMES AND TWO TIMERS AND OLD
FRIENDS AND OLD TALES AND FRESH PER-
SPECTIVES AND ON BEHALF
OF MY YOUNGER SELF WHOM I SEE LOOKING
UPWARDS AND MY OLDER SELF WHOM I FEEL
SMILING DOWN AND PROCLAIMING
REGRETS ON YOUR DEATH BED OR DEATH ON
YOUR CURRENT BED
EITHER WAY YOU MAKE IT TO THE END OF A
SENTENCE

WHICH IS ONLY THAT
IF YOU SO CHOOSE.

I'M WRITING BECAUSE IT ISN'T DONE ENOUGH
EVEN IF IT'S DONE TOO MUCH
AND YET ENOUGH IS WHAT WE ARE
NOT ALWAYS HOW WE FEEL
I'M WRITING TO ASK QUESTIONS
I'D NEVER THOUGHT TO HAVE ASKED
TO QUESTION ANSWERS I'D NEVER ASKED TO
BELIEVE
I'M WRITING TO BE HOLY TO BE SPIRIT AND
SPEAKER AND THE SPOKEN TO AND THE
WORDS SPOKEN TOO
YOU UNDERSTAND
REALLY THIS MEANS
I WANT TO WANT NOTHING
AND BECOME EVERYTHING
WITH YOU AND YOU AND YOU
AND ALL OF US HERE
CREATING FREELY AND BLEEDING
OVER BARRIERS AND SLIPPING INTO THE BIND

122

ONLY TO RELEASE OURSELVES BY OUR OWN
HAND WITH OUR OWN MIND
TEARING OUT & MAKING UP
FREELY AND WITHOUT REGARD
FOR THE MATERIAL
IN REGARDS TO THIS MATERIAL,
THE BOOK

Also Out On Far West

farwestpress.com

CPSIA information can be obtained
at www.ICGtesting.com
Printed in the USA
BVHW030807010721
610937BV00002B/71